Confessions of a People Pleaser

M.J. Farrell

BookLeaf Publishing

India | USA | UK

Presentation by *BookLeaf Publishing*

Web: www.bookleafpub.com

E-mail: info@bookleafpub.com

ISBN:9789358316032

First edition 2024

DEDICATION

For all the beautiful people who bear the cost of faithful living, we will still love with our all, enduring and unwavering. May these pages reflect the depth of your spirit and the power of your love. Let us learn to do so wisely.

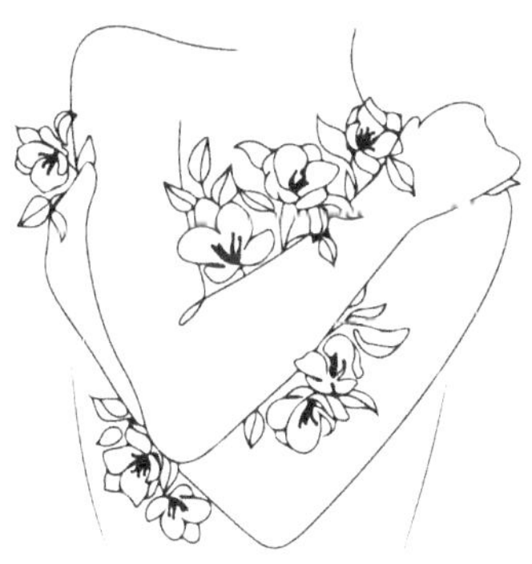

PREFACE

While working aboard a family cruise line, I found myself engrossed in a conversation with friends about a recent phone call from home. The topic of getting a tattoo had crossed my mind, and while I leaned toward the idea, the disapproving reactions of my beloved family members left me with doubts. Little did I anticipate that this seemingly minor incident would ignite a profound revelation about myself: I am a people pleaser. I realized I valued the approval and peace of mind within my family more than I craved the simple addition of ink on my wrist.

Sharing this revelation with my friends, they too began to share their own experiences, and together we humorously concluded that anyone working for a certain magical rodent must inherently be a people pleaser. As we laughed, the truth of our revelation struck home. I grappled with the question of how to navigate life with this newfound self-awareness and the thought of how to protect ourselves from those who might exploit our vulnerabilities that caused many sleepless nights. In the quiet hours of dawn, the seeds of this confessional story began to sprout.

As you read along, I hope you find inspiration in your own journey of self-discovery and remember that you are deserving of love, respect, and an authentically fulfilling life.

Table of Contents

The Altruist's Prelude

In the dance of empathy, a silent call,
A yearning to uplift, to help them stand tall.
A lamppost in the shadows, burning bright,
Guiding others through the darkest night.

A gallery of smiles, a purpose clear,
To dry the tears and quell the fear.
In pleasing others, a joy unfolds,
As hearts connect and stories are told.

The allure of altruism, a comforting embrace,
A desire to bring solace to every face.
In this tapestry of kindness woven fine,
A sense of purpose, like vintage wine.

So, embark with me on this heartfelt quest,
To explore the realms of giving our best.
In the art of pleasing, where intentions shine,
Let this collection unravel, a journey divine.

Nice

I've discovered our secret
What makes us tick
It's nice to know I am not alone
That we all fit neatly into this dysfunction

My friends, we don't just want people to like us
We need it, feed on it
We need them to think well of us
We need them to miss us.

Trust me, I know this is a disease
I'd rather one person desire the real me
But I was raised to be nice
So if all don't think I am, I've failed

Oh friends, those caught in this addiction
How unfortunate it is for us to be
We end up appeasing and attracting
Narcissists and abusers

They have preyed on our weakness
And mastered how to subdue us
In the hardship of leaving our dependent
enslavement
We run the risk of using their tactics

My dear Hansel and Gretel
You do not need to breadcrumb
Or manipulate with emotions
It was wrong that you were exploited, but don't
become the witch

You are too nice to fall into this

Fitting room

Who will I be today?

Shall I be the innocent
Dressed in soft pinks and whites
Fitting into a world of naive hopes and
simplicities
Of teddy bears and safety blankets?

Or do I go the dangerous confident red
The one of passion and fire
Bold, brave
The world of lust and love (or is real love white
like gowns?)

I could breathe in and wear the greens
Fall into peace and rest
I can be amongst the grass and trees
That will long outlive me

Does the day call for joy and heroism
Of gold and sunshine
Or is it the bittersweet blues
Sadness so large it fills both the ocean and skies

Shall I be black-death
Dark and cold as my soul
Or royal purple, something I will never know
Though I dream of a king to make me whole

Am I barren and old
An orange dried out desert
Sun scorched
With only enough life to struggle to each new
dawn

Am I the muted miry dust and clay,
Grey and lifeless
Or young pastel, or vibrant perfect hues
Where do I fit today?

Either way the spanx shall contort my size
The mind will be forced through the turtleneck
Which shall choke my voice from escaping
Keeping up my perfect disguise

I smell danger

Little girl fell down
The rabbit hole
And being in Rome
Did as the Romans do

She feasted when they said eat
She drank when they said drink

She restrained from succumbing at first
For she didn't belong here
But time made her heart and mind divorce
So her body could sleep

She played when they said play
She lost when they demanded she lose

She was happy
That's all they wanted for her
Little girl had made that
Her new year's resolution

She smiled when they said smile
She dressed as they told her to dress

She met the hatter and march hare
Who lavished her with treats
The cheshire cat let her stroke him
And purred with such bliss

She laughed when they said laugh
She bowed when they said bow

But through hazy dreams she recalled
A king who lifted her to receive such bows
Who wanted so much more
Then a smile stitched poorly on her face

Should she climb out of the dirt?
Should she flee from her wonderland?

Please still like me

I know now
What my mother meant
When she labelled me a flirt

It's not what she thought
Though
I am something much worse

A flirt knows she is seducing

A me, well,
She just doesn't want to lose what she had
Even if she doesn't want it.

So she keeps you
Just close enough;
A dog on a lead

To fulfil her corrupt need of dependency

S.A.D

As an insignificant
Blade of grass
Needs sunlight

So do I

I need the sunshine
To put a smile
On my face

I need it as much as I need your approval

When the sky is blue
The sun a perfect temperature
I can shine at my bubbly self-love

But when the clouds roll in, I wither

I cannot handle the suns rejection
Much like how I can't handle yours
Why I can only be sustained by
acknowledgement

So, sun, do not turn your face from me

Please see what I do for you
Always kind, sweet and helpful
Bending under other's feet when you shine
happily upon them

Crash

I'm not sure if our language truly grasps
A name
For what we both shared and felt

This connection
This magnetic pull
When your gaze met mine

It's not mere lust
Or a fleeting desire
It runs deeper than to physically admire

As if our meeting was fated
For our souls to stand bare
Unburdened by shame when we converse

You sought my company willingly
I responded with a smile
You seemed to understand my essence without
words

A connection
Twin flame
Soulmate—these terms don't entirely fit

Our meeting was happenstance
Yet it feels like a dream
Our energy, a volatile spark,

Eager to burst into flames,
But the constraints of society
Kept our physicality at bay

So our minds danced instead,
The cadence of your intellect
Intertwining with mine

The space between us diminished
With each shared thought,
Each shared breath

I've encountered this before
This soul-deep longing,
It's an undeniable knowing

As though we've known one another
In some distant time
Or perhaps we're fragments of each other's souls

Could these be eye contracts?
Forged across history—friends,
Sisters, brothers, lovers?

It's filled with awe and chaos
Simultaneously graceful and wild
It inspires reverence and devotion

Even the expression
Of this spiritual connection
Proves elusive to articulate

My attempts fall short
Of capturing the warmth and fire
Radiated by the aura of our bond

All I know is
I miss staring into your eyes
And the way your hand lingered after a high five

Sumptuous

How hungrily she consumed
Your whispers on her neck
And intoxicated by your promise
Caved to kissing you before knowing your name

How she boasted
To any ear that cared to hear
Of your blessings, kindness and physicality
Upon her heart and flesh

How the touch of your skin
Spiked her brain
And spiralling the lovers jabbed the needle
Without shame

How the possession of you
Absorbed her doing
And her family, friends, dreams and
Even God took the back seat of what she had
once nurtured

How the foolishness she felt
When you were with someone else
Filled her mind with ugliness
Longing to steal you back

How she woke up from too real
A dream of the two intertwined
The thought tipping her over and over
Desperate to be fully enraptured

How she wishes she'd known the outcome
Before this all begun
At least she knows now
Only God can be trusted

The ABC's of peacekeeping

A tranquil lighthouse stands firm
Against the raging storming seas
A guiding beam of hope and calm
Amongst treacherous rocks of conflict

But so few see the cracks
Beneath their serene facade, the weight they
Bear, the toll of protecting peace.
Be piteous of this soldier; their pain is an eternal
wound

Crushed by the tides of grief and torture
Chosen or sacrificed to be someone else's anchor
Calamity drags their hearts to the depths of the
ocean
Causing them to give you their last breath of air

No

In the realm of decisions,
A struggle resides,
A challenge to utter the word denied

Bound by the fear of disappointing another,
Unable to refuse,
My voice does smother

A prisoner of yes,
My boundaries unseen,
Yearning for the strength to break this routine

Opinion

I remember the first time I rebelled
I crossed my arms
Defiant
My mother commanded I apologise

After a pause I complied

And the second time
I skipped class
Elated
But my teacher caught me

I cried for forgiveness

More recently I wanted something taboo
But the ravens plucked my feathers
Distorting
The line between rebellion and truth

I considered that some fights aren't worth
winning

Mask

Amidst the masquerade, the true self unfolds,
Hidden desires, finally told.
Beneath the ruffles and lace's allure,
Lies a world where temptations endure.

Pearls and rubies, seducing wealth,
Conceal the cravings, and feign a need for stealth.
Gloves and heels, a facade of grace,
Cloaking the darkness, the desired embrace.

In this realm of colours and disguise,
Leering animal skulls meet searching eyes.
Grotesque costumes, a twisted charade,
Unveiling the vices, no longer afraid.

Demonic gargoyles, guardians of sin,
Witness the dances where souls cave in.
In sport and jest, they revel and sway,
Delighting the flesh, in this wicked display.

Illusory

I was once stuck in a world of glitz and glam
Of costumes and rubies
Innocent strong men
And princesses fair

In this daydream
One felt bold and brave
One could adventure, and be rewarded
With the trust and faith of true love's kiss

In the straight jacket's embrace
I felt safe but reality has to burn
The safety blanket of dysfunction

Like flipping into the upside down
What once shimmered turned to ash
The hero a villain
And love was labelled to be cruel

Out of 'bravery' the princess said yes to every
Depraved request
Surely if she were meek and mild
The 'love making' could be a safety net?
Not so,

Instead, she finally left

To live up to

In Proverbs' wisdom, she's a beacon bright,
A woman strong, a radiant guiding light.
With noble virtues, her heart's a precious gem,
The Proverbs 31 woman, she shines within.

This is what I've been conditioned to be
A standard too high to keep, I flee
Shame fills me as I stumble
I fear the Lord, but unlike 31, I tremble

How could he love me
She who does not work as the busy bee
Who loves her sleep ins
And is too vain, regards her double chins

She craves strength and dignity
Yet crumbles when a boy calls her pretty
Her time wasted on self care
Instead of ensuring her husband's reputation is
fair

I try to be these things
Truly, I long for my words to bring wisdom, like
pearls on a string
I endeavour for kindness to flow from my
tongue
But there will never be songs about me sung

I do not despise 31
She is beautiful and like me, lots of fun
But her behaviour is not just for women to aspire
to
No, young men, this proverb is for you too

Has the penny dropped
Has your heart sort of stopped
Because so many of you boys, do not see
yourself as God's bride.
Perhaps you are too full of pride

Fear not, we all fall short
But maybe now my life will not be such sport
And your expectations of your future wife
Will be salted with patience, as we all live a
different life

Puppeteer

Just give me a second master
To change into the correct costume
I can't clean your mess
While wearing this wedding dress

I need my scrubs
If I am to tend to your wounds
And hand me my notepad
As I fix your grievances

Here is your paper bag
Stuffed full of nutrients and yummy food
Let me kiss you before you go
Surely I do not embarrass you or your friends

Shall I wear the white or red tonight?
Or am I to bare the hospital gown,
Pushing out your descendants
And applaud you with your new conquest

Am I yet to earn your favour,
Am I able to eat the crumbs at your feet?
You need a foot rub first, well of course,
After all

I aim to please

Power over me

26

Awaking from a hazy dream I choke on reality's smoke.
Where is my torch or guiding light to clarity and freedom?
Can I not see what has been clear since creation?
I've claimed so, I believe and have been believing.
I'm left baffled by a control that seems so untimely.
Perhaps David Bowie keeps me in this messy maze?

Camouflage

A chameleon within, I adapt to others' whims,
A willow twisting and darting, escaping their
demands, and sins.

Bending over backwards, a weasel, I writhe
Escaping the predicaments of their requests
design.

Like a leopard, my spots conceal the strife,
In plain view, I navigate this complex life.

Performing like a retriever for their treats,
Seeking their approval, my self-esteem depletes.

Flittering from one to the next I roam,
Nectar-seeking, making their wishes my home.

Shall I be your monkey, earning your coin,
Dancing to your tune, my identity purloined?

Will satisfaction dawn only when I roost on your
shoulder,
My vivid hues silent, while I regurgitate your
discordant splutter?

I'm tired of being the swan in this ballet,
My effort and struggle hidden beneath the
waterway

This lapdog yearns to recall her ancestral roots,
But due to the daunting path of the lone wolf,
stays put.

Slave Force

I do this
At work constantly.
Focused on diligently striving for perfection
That I end up doing the work of 10 men;
Paid at 75% of one man's wage.

I do this
With a smile on my face
Pleased with the minimal praise
That my slavery warrants me,
And shamed when I don't meet my own
unachievable expectations.

I do this
With superiority in my stride
Perplexed how the others have not contorted
their lives
Like a rat desperate for food.
I am jealous they aren't treated like vermin; like
me.

Is this war?

It's rather amusing
How simplicity is never quite
Simple

Creating clear boundaries,
Drawing resolute lines in the sand,
Waver, they get muddied and twisted.

I wonder who's to blame
I point the finger inward
For not defending my boundaries with resolve.

I established them clearly from the start,
With transparency and mutual understanding,
Striving to preserve a just harmony.

But my eagerness to please you,
Rendered my rules a mockery,
Allowing you to encroach on my territory.

In the world at large, such trespass is a call to
arms,
Yet in relationships, why does it differ?
Why must I surrender my very soul?

It's not all bad

You are emulating
What is noble and best
A beacon you stand
Offering a safe warm place

You want to be hope
You want to nurture and guide
You want to dry tears
And be a place for others to hide

It's beautiful
How you strive to make others smile
That the peace of their hearts
Is of the highest importance

You are wonderful.
You cower from such praise
You do this for them
Not for the accolades

Don't lose this compassion
There's nothing wrong with the way you are
It's ideal even to help heal scars
But be wise, as there are snakes lying in wait

Resistance

I hate this feeling
After I've committed to change
That in my formed decision
You feel the need to shut me down

I'm trying to be strong
And learn to stand firm
But when you do this
I'm led to feel you hate me

This may not be true
But it becomes apparent
You don't trust me
Or my authenticity

Reflective shadows

I let you talk me out
Of my righteous disagreement
Because I wanted you to see
I'm reasonable

But I shouldn't have to play tiptoeing games

The truth is I was right
And you crawled back to your own vomit
Don't cry to me
When tragedy repeats itself

I have foresight and wisdom you could never
attain

You let a false sense of failure
Lead you to further pain
In you I see a past mirror
My heart dependant on another

I pray that I won't slip back, that I won't be like
you

This is the greatest risk I run
Afterall, isn't that exactly what I did
I wanted your approval
More than listening to my gut

The voice of the universe dwells in wisdom
there

Fortress

Walls build up
High parapets
Guarding the fragile treasure within

Suitors come
Casting doubts in the ruler
Their charm questions the need for such
protections

Guilt forms
As the gnawing vultures
Pick at his defences

No longer believing a need to conceal
He partakes of their wine
His stupor making him blind

Exposed, the secret is destroyed and abandoned.
Cradling the shattered blessing, The King
rebuilds his towers
Stronger and resolute, against future descent.

Priorities

She lost her footing, I witnessed,
Her mind unravelling before my eyes.
But to you she was perfectly fine.

I watched her selflessness, repeatedly,
Placing others and your feelings above her own.

All in the hope you'd come to cherish her.

But you favoured those who rejected you
instead,
Though you profess impartiality,
Your people-pleasing bent your values.

She yearns for just one thing,
A smile when you see her face.

But you respond with rebukes and scorn.

Injection room

I am the worst
People praise me
'You are so strong, so brave, so fun, so
nice'
But I am weak, a leech
Feeding on acceptance and approval
My drug, my addiction
Shot straight through my veins

There is so much wrong with me

This is what I say to myself
To keep me humble
To not be vain
But instead, it deteriorates my brain

I say I have no personality
But then how can I connect with you
I say no one could want to be my friend
But then how can I connect with you?

I've had to learn that my villain is a liar

I am brave
I am intelligent, kind, fun
I am worthy of love

I am not superior, but I am also not inferior

I make errors
Sometimes quite a few before I actually learn
But as I keep growing,
I lose my drug dependency

Practice

"No"

A simple word, but heavy with meaning,
A boundary I've set, please start heeding.

I asked you to halt, but you persisted,
Trust was tested, and you resisted.

I offered a second chance, forgiveness extended,
Yet lacking respect for me, you defended.

My choice isn't a punishment, it's wisdom, you
see,
Please understand, respect my decree.

My feelings matter, you can't deny,
But you continue to disregard my cry.

So, for now, we part our ways,
Until you learn to mend your errant ways.

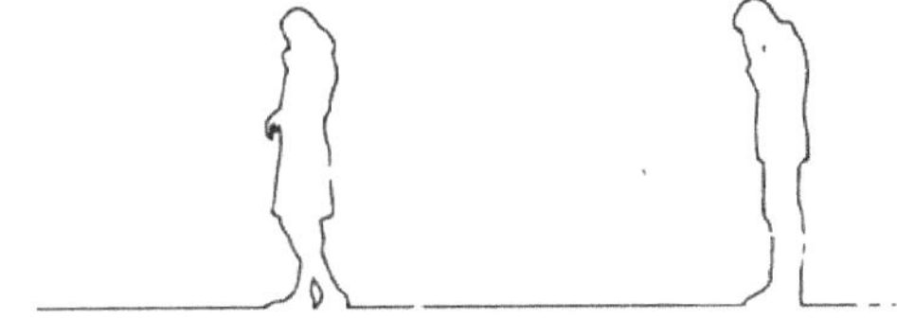

"No" means "No," it's not up for debate,
Stop pushing boundaries, it's time to relate.

"No"

Watch my tongue

Yesterday, I wounded a stranger's soul,
Unwittingly revealing a stone-cold heart,
A brat without grace, patience my distant goal.

But that's not who I am, though she'll never know,
I presented myself as a pompous airhead,
A facade of my true self, lost in ego's show.

I've been reckless, carelessly wielding words,
Unaware of the wounds my sword might bear,
In my quest for healing, the infection silently stirs.

They say life's a journey, progress mixed with regress,
I'm determined to hold on to the changes I'm making,
But I can't be careless, thoughtless; to these I confess.

I want my life to embody love's warm embrace,
Even if I'm opinionated,
I must learn to deflect wrath's bitter face

Entwined with you

Once, I stood resolute in my care for others,
A lamppost, a lighthouse, a fortress protector.
But at the crossroads, I had to contemplate,
The need to tend their fires or my own fate.

I've devoted my life to others' safety and delight,
Surrendered my voice to ensure laughter's light.
Now, I see the path veering to the right,
An opportunity to nurture my soul, to take flight.

I've traversed the broad road of pleasing,
It's time to embrace the 'me' I've been
concealing.
In setting boundaries and practising self-care,
I find an unshakable strength beyond compare.

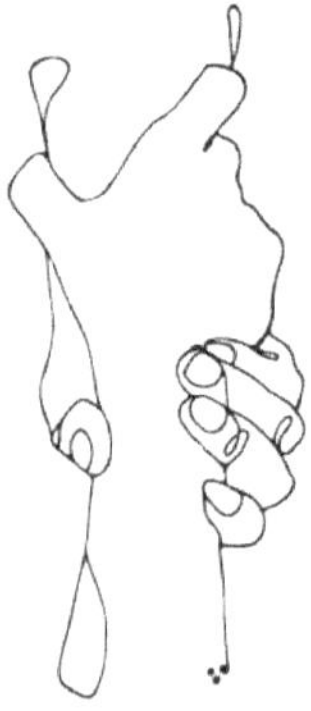

So, as the final verse in this humble tale,
I stand for others, but myself, I unveil.
With love for all and a heart that's kind,
I tread a path where self and others entwine.

The journey unfolds, with wisdom as my guide,
Balancing kindness and the care I provide.
In self-discovery, a beautiful rebirth,
Where the value of all is found, along with my
own self-worth.

ACKNOWLEDGEMENT

Thank You

As I come to the end of this journey, I am overwhelmed with gratitude for all those who have supported and inspired me along the way. To my family, who provided unwavering encouragement and love, and to mum, especially for reading through draft after draft, offering feedback and support. This work is as much yours as it is mine.

To my friends, whose conversations and laughter breathed life into these pages, thank you. I could not have succeeded in this without you.

I am deeply appreciative of the countless hours of dedication from my colleagues Shikha, Ranjana and Lavleen at Bookleaf Publishing, who helped shape and refine this work into its final form. I appreciated the challenges set forth by the company, and the encouragement to collaborate in part with GPT-3. Due to my dyslexia, I found it helpful for the first draft editing and getting inspiration. I take ultimate responsibility for the content of this publication. To the artists and designers who contributed their talents to bring this book to life, your creativity has added a layer of beauty that words alone could not achieve.

I cannot express my gratitude enough to Heba Edwards for her superb photography skills and our deep chats over cups of tea. You are an exceptional woman and I am so pleased to know you and call you a friend.

To my readers, your curiosity, engagement, and feedback have been invaluable. Your presence on this journey is the ultimate reward. I will never forget the kind words and reviews you have given me. I hope we can all meet for a cup of tea and catch up as old friends.

And finally, to all those who believe in the power of storytelling, may we continue to find wonder and wisdom in the pages of books. Your support has made this endeavour possible.

With heartfelt gratitude,

M.J. Farrell